Bon A

KU-167-051

PASTAS

Foreword

Naturally there are many Italian recipes in
this book but to give an international flavour there are recipes from the exotic East
and some traditional specialities originating
from the Bavarian region of Germany.

Do be careful to follow one type of measure
throughout the recipe. The three measures
given are Metric, Imperial and American
(cups). Where American ingredients differ
from English, the American name has been
put in brackets.

All recipes are for four people unless otherwise stated.

Bon Appétit.

Tagliatelle with chervil sauce

Ingredients

225g/8oz/¹⁄₂lb tagliatelle
40g/1¹⁄₂oz/3tbs butter
275g/10oz/10oz tomatoes,
blanched, skinned, seeded
300ml/¹⁄₂pt/¹⁄₄cups sour cream
nutmeg, grated
1x15ml/1tbs/1tbs chervil, chopped
Parmesan cheese, grated
chervil leaves
sprig of basil or parsley

Method

1. Put the noodles into a pan containing 1 ½ litres/2 ½ pts/5 ¾ cups of boiling, salted water, return to the boil and cook for 8

- 10 minutes until tender, stirring occasionally. Pour the noodles into a strainer, rinse with cold water and drain.
2. Melt the butter in the pan, add the noodles and mix thoroughly.
3. Add the chopped tomatoes and the sour cream to the noodles and heat whilst stirring.
4. Shortly before serving stir in salt, pepper, nutmeg and chervil. Flavour to taste with Parmesan cheese. Sprinkle with chervil leaves and garnish with a sprig of basil or parsley.

Tagliatelle with mussels

Ingredients

225g/8oz/½lb tagliatelle
1x15ml/1tbs/1tbs salad oil
1 - 2 cloves garlic, peeled and crushed
225g/8oz/½lb mushrooms
handful parsley, chopped
500g/1lb/1lb can or jar of mussels
50g/2oz/4 tbs butter
salt and pepper
onion powder

Method

1. Put the tagliatelle into 2 litres/3 ½ pts/9 cups of boiling, salted water, add the oil and boil for about 15 minutes until tender, stirring occasionally. Pour the noodles into a strainer, rinse with cold water and leave to drain.
2. Put noodles into oven-proof dish, melt a dab of butter and stir through the noodles.
3. Wash and slice the mushrooms. Drain the mussels and reserve the liquid.
4. Melt the butter in a pan and add garlic. Add the mushrooms and parsley, simmer for about 5 minutes then add a little of the liquid drained from the mussels. Cover the pan and simmer for about 10 minutes.
5. Add the mussels and heat through, then add salt, pepper and onion powder to taste. Ladle the sauce over the noodles in a warm serving dish. Serve at once.

Macaroni and tagliatelle

Macaroni salad

(6 portions)

Ingredients

100g/4oz/¼lb long thick macaroni
100g/4oz/¼lb German sausage
½ cucumber
2 tomatoes, blanched, skinned, seeded and diced
2 onions
100g/4oz/¼lb Emmenthal cheese
½ head of endive or, approx 175g/6oz/6oz Chinese cabbage

For the dressing:
4x15ml/4tbs/5tbs salad oil
2x15ml/2tbs/3tbs vinegar
2x15ml/2tbs/3tbs white wine
1x5ml/1tsp/1tsp strong mustard
salt and pepper
sugar
cayenne pepper
2x15ml/2tbs/3tbs chopped dill

Method

1. To make the salad: Break the macaroni into lengths of about 2 cm (1''), drop into 1 litre/1 ¾pts/4 ½ cups of salted water and bring to the boil. Boil for about 15 minutes until tender, stirring occasionally. Pour into a strainer, rinse with cold water and leave to drain well.
2. Remove the skin, slice the sausage and halve the slices.
3. Wash and dry the cucumber, cut in half lengthways, remove the seeds and cut into slices.
4. Peel the onions and cut into rings. Cut the Emmenthal cheese into strips.
5. Wash and slice the endive or Chinese cabbage into small pieces and make sure it is well drained. Add tomatoes, toss all together.
6. To make the dressing: Mix the salad oil, vinegar, white wine and mustard. Add salt, pepper, sugar and cayenne pepper to taste, then pour over the salad and toss well together. Salt, pepper or sugar may be added to taste.
Finally, sprinkle with dill.

Italian salad

Ingredients

100g/4oz/¼lb thin long macaroni
100g/4oz/¼lb cooked beef
100g/4oz/¼lb boiled ham
225 g/8oz/½lb tomatoes, blanched, skinned, seeded, diced
1 green pepper
2 gherkins
2x5ml/2tsp/2tsp capers

For the dressing:
1x15ml/1tbs/2tbs salad oil
2x15ml/2tbs/3tbs vinegar
3x15/3tbs/4tbs cream
salt and pepper, and sugar
1x15ml/1tbs/2tbs parsley,
chopped
1x15ml/1tbs/2tbs chives,
chopped

Garnish:
Slices of hardboiled egg and
parsley

Method

1. To make the salad: Break the macaroni into pieces about
   2.5 cm (1'') long and place in 1 litre/1 ¾pts/4 ½ cups of
   boiling, salted water. Boil for about 15 minutes, stirring
   occasionally. Pour into a strainer, rinse with cold water and
   leave to drain.
2. Cut the ham and beef into strips.
3. Cut the green pepper in half. Remove stalk, core, pith and
   seeds and cut into thin strips. Cut the gherkins into cubes and
   add capers, tomatoes, and mix well together.
4. To make the dressing: Mix the salad oil and vinegar with the
   cream and season with salt, pepper and sugar to taste.
5. Stir the parsley and chives through the dressing and pour over
   the salad. Toss until all ingredients are coated with dressing.

Fettucine with smoked salmon

Ingredients

400g/14oz/14oz fettucine

For the sauce:
275g/10oz/10oz tomatoes, blan-
ched, skinned, seeded and
finely diced
100g/4oz/¼lb smoked salmon (sliced)
2 cloves garlic, peeled, crushed
75g/3oz/6tbs black olives
3x15ml/3tbs/4tbs olive oil
300ml/½pt/1 ¼ cups sour cream
salt and pepper
1x5ml/1tsp/1tsp mint leaves, chopped
1x2.5ml/½tsp/½tsp oregano leaves

Method

1. Cut the salmon into thin strips. Remove the stones and cut olives into small pieces.

2. Heat the oil in a pan and add the garlic. Add the salmon and olives, retaining some for garnishing. Stir and cook gently for 2 - 3 minutes.

3. Add the sour cream, stir well then add the tomato, heat. Season. Stir in the mint and oregano leaves and keep the sauce hot.

4. Put the fettucine into 3 litres/5 ½pts/12 cups of boiling, salted water. Return to the boil and boil for 8 - 10 minutes until tender, stirring occasionally. Pour into a strainer, rinse with cold water and leave to drain.

5. Arrange the pasta in a serving dish, pour the sauce on the top and decorate with remaining slices of salmon and black olives.

Noodles Tyrolienne

Ingredients

1kg/2lbs/2lbs white cabbage
2 large onions, peeled and chopped
75g/3oz/6tbs lard
salt and pepper
225g/8oz/½lb fettucine
1 thick slice of mild Continental sausage

Method

1. Slice finely, wash and drain the cabbage.
2. Heat the fat in a pan (preferably cast iron). Add the onions and cabbage, and season. Cook for about 25 minutes, stirring constantly until the vegetables are light golden brown.
3. Place the fettucine in 2 litres/3 ½pts/9 cups boiling, salted water. Boil for about 15 minutes until cooked, stirring occasionally. Pour the pasta into a strainer, rinse with cold water and leave to drain.
4. Cut the sausage in half, cut into strips and add with the pasta to the cabbage. Stir while heating and season to taste.

Macaroni with garlic and olive oil
(4 - 5 portions)

Ingredients

4 cloves garlic, peeled and crushed
8x15ml/8tbs/½ cup olive oil, salt
2 red peppers
4x15ml/4tbs/5tbs parsley, chopped
500g/1lb/1lb macaroni

Method

1. Heat the olive oil. Fry the garlic until golden brown and season with salt.

2. Halve the peppers, remove seeds and dice the peppers.
3. Add the peppers and parsley to the garlic. Fry and keep hot.
4. Put macaroni into 3 litres/5½pts/12 cups of boiling, salted water. Boil for 10 - 12 minutes until tender. Pour into a strainer, rinse with cold water, drain, then mix with the garlic sauce and serve at once.

Macaroni with garlic and olive oil

Macaroni with piquant cheese

(2 - 4 portions)

Ingredients

225g/8oz/¹⁄₂lb macaroni
2x15ml/2tbs/3tbs soft butter
225/8oz/¹⁄₂lb low fat cheese
120ml/4fl.oz/¹⁄₂ cup cream
40g/1¹⁄₂oz/3 tbs Parmesan cheese, grated
salt and pepper
paprika

Method

Preheat oven to 225°C/450°F/Gas 7.
1. Put the macaroni into 2 litres/3 ¹⁄₂pts/9 cups of boiling, salted water. Boil for about 10 minutes until tender, stirring occasionally. Pour into a strainer, rinse with cold water and leave to drain.
2. Mix the butter, low fat cheese and cream together. Add the Parmesan cheese. Season with salt, pepper and paprika and stir carefully through the macaroni.
3. Put the mixture into a buttered oven-proof dish and place in centre of preheated oven. Cook for approximately 5 - 10 minutes.

Tomato tortiglioni soufflé

Ingredients

175g/6oz/6oz green tortiglioni
750g/1¹⁄₂lb/1¹⁄₂lb tomatoes, blanched, skinned, sliced
150g/6oz/6oz boiled ham, sliced
3 eggs

120ml/4fl.oz/¹⁄₂ cup milk
2x15ml/2tbs/3tbs chives, chopped
2x15ml/2tbs/3tbs chives, chopped
100g/4oz/¹⁄₄lb cheese, sliced

Method

Preheat oven to 200°C/400°F/Gas 6.
1. Put the tortiglioni into 1½ litres/2½pts/6¾ cups of boiling, salted water. Boil for about 8 minutes until tender, stirring occasionally. Pour into a strainer, rinse with cold water and leave to drain.
2. Cut the ham into small pieces. Grease an oven-proof dish and fill alternately with slices of tomato, ham and the pasta.
3. Beat the eggs, add the milk. Stir in the parsley and chives and season. Pour the mixture over the pasta.
4. Arrange the cheese slices on top of the pasta and place in the centre of the oven for approximately 20 minutes until golden brown.

Tomato tortiglioni soufflé

Macaroni with paprika-fig sauce

Ingredients

6 green and red peppers
1 head of celery
4x15ml/4tbs/¼ cup olive oil
salt and pepper
3 ripe figs
400g/14oz/14oz thin, long macaroni

Method

1. Place macaroni in 3 litres/5½pts/12 cups of boiling, salted water. Boil for about 12 minutes until tender, stirring occasionally. Pour into a strainer, rinse with cold water and leave until well drained.

2. To make the sauce: Halve the peppers. Remove the seeds, pith and core, and wash. Prepare and wash the celery.
Cut both ingredients into dice.

3. Heat the olive oil in a pan. Add the vegetables, fry gently for 10 - 15 minutes, stirring occasionally. If required, add a few spoonfuls of water. Season.

4. Peel the figs, cut into small pieces and stir through the vegetables. Keep hot.

5. Put the macaroni into a warm serving dish, arrange the paprika-fig sauce on top and serve at once.

Buttered macaroni

Ingredients

175g/6oz/6oz long, thin macaroni
2x15ml/2tbs/3tbs butter
grated Parmesan cheese, to taste
pepper or paprika

Method

1. Break the macaroni into finger-length pieces and sprinkle into 1½litres /2½pts/6 cups of boiling, salted water. Boil for about 12 minutes until tender. Pour into a strainer, rinse with cold water and leave to drain.
2. Melt butter and stir through the macaroni.
3. Mix cheese with pepper or paprika and sprinkle over the macaroni.

Venetian salad

Ingredients

225g/8oz/½lb long macaroni,
cooked al dente
100g/4oz/¼lb gherkins
50g/2oz/2oz Parma ham
100g/4oz/¼lb salami
100g/4oz/¼lb Emmenthal cheese
4 tomatoes, blanched, skinned,
seeded
4 sour apples

For the dressing:
3x15ml/3tbs/4tbs tomato
ketchup (catsup)
2x15ml/2tbs/3tbs salad oil
2x15ml/2tbs/3tbs wine
vinegar
salt and pepper
1-2 sprigs parsley, chopped
1-2 sprigs chives, finely
chopped

Method

1. Break the macaroni into bite-size pieces. Cut the gherkins, ham, salami and Emmenthal into strips.

2. Peel and core the apples, cut into quarters. Cut tomatoes and apples into strips.
3. To make the dressing: Mix tomato ketchup with oil and vinegar. Season. Mix in parsley and chives and combine dressing with the salad. Leave until well absorbed.

Venetian salad

Vegetable soup with macaroni

Ingredients

500g/1lb/1lb marrowbone
4 peppercorns
2 dried, seeded chillies
1 bay leaf
500g/1lb/1lb chuck steak
500g/1lb/1lb breast of chicken
500g/1lb/1lb carrots
100g/4oz/¼lb celeriac, peeled and diced
500g/1lb/1lb Brussels sprouts
100g/4oz/¼lb short cut (elbow) macaroni
salt and pepper
parsley, chopped

Method

1. Rinse the marrowbone. Put into 2 litres/3 ½ pts/9 cups of salted water together with the peppercorns, chillies and the bay leaf. Bring to the boil and skim off the foam.
2. Rinse and dry the chuck steak. Add to the broth and simmer for about 1 ¼ hours. Rinse the chicken breast, add to the broth, bring to the boil and simmer for another 45 minutes.
3. Remove the meat and marrowbone from the broth. Remove any skin or fat and cut the meat into cubes. Sieve the broth and keep warm.
4. Scrape and dice the carrots and celeriac. Prepare the Brussels sprouts. Add vegetables to the broth. Bring to the boil and cook for 20 minutes until tender.
5. Put the macaroni into 1 ½ litres/2 ½pts/6 cups of boiling, salted water, stirring occasionally. Boil for about 15 minutes until tender. Pour into a strainer, rinse with cold water and leave to drain.
6. Put the meat and macaroni into the soup and heat up quickly. Season the soup and sprinkle with parsley.

Home made noodles

Ingredients

225g/8oz/¹⁄₂lb plain flour (all purpose flour)
1x5ml/1tsp/1tsp salt
2 eggs
*2-3x15ml/2-3tbs/3-4tbs water **

Method

1. Sieve the flour onto the table or pastry board and make a hollow in the middle of the flour. Mix the eggs with the salt and water.
2. Pour the mixture into the hollow and using some of the flour, make a thick paste. Then, working from the centre outwards, quickly knead all the ingredients into a smooth dough.
3. If the dough is sticky, add some flour. Divide the dough into 4. Roll out the dough to noodle thickness.
4. Lay the sheets of dough on flour dusted cloths to dry. When the sheets of dough are so dry that they no longer stick together but also do not break, they can be cut in the desired length and width. Expose the strips of noodle to the air until they are completely dry.

*   With large eggs take the lesser amount of water and with small eggs take the greater amount of water.

Fettucine au gratin

Ingredients

225/8oz/¹⁄₂lb fettucine
2 onions, peeled, diced
1 clove garlic, peeled, crushed
1x15ml/1tbs/2tbs butter
500g/1lb/1lb minced
pork and beef
salt and pepper

paprika
1x5ml/1tsp/1tsp thyme, dried
500g/1lb/1lb tomatoes,
blanched, skinned, diced
100g/4oz/¹⁄₄lb Parmesan or
Cheddar cheese, grated

Method

Preheat oven to 190°C/375°F/Gas 5.
1. Put the fettucine into 1 ½ litres/2 ½ pts/6 cups salted water, cook for about 8 minutes, stirring occasionally. Pour through a strainer, rinse with cold water and leave to drain.
2. Melt the butter in a pan and gently fry the onions and garlic until transparent. Add the meat and cook while stirring, breaking up any lumps. Season with salt and pepper, paprika and thyme. Stir in tomatoes. Simmer for about 5 minutes.
3. Put ⅔rds of the pasta into a greased, oven-proof dish. Add the meat mixture and cover with the rest of the pasta. Sprinkle the cheese over the top and dot with a little butter.
4. Cook in preheated oven for 35 minutes. Serve with fresh green salad.

Fettucine au gratin

Tagliatelle with seafood

Ingredients

500g/1lb/1lb tagliatelle
3x15ml/3tbs/4tbs butter

For the mussel sauce:
1 onion
1 clove garlic, peeled and crushed
1x15ml/1tbs/2tbs salad oil
120ml/¼pt/½ cup white wine
1 bay leaf
salt and pepper
300g/10oz/10oz fresh mussels
(in their shells)
500g/1lb/1lb tomatoes, blan-
ched, skinned, seeded and diced
225g/8oz/½ lb mussels (potted)
100g/4oz/¼lb frozen shrimps, defrosted
1x15ml/1tbs/2tbs capers
parsley, chopped

Method

1. Put the pasta in 4 litres/5 ¼ pts/12 cups of boiling, salted water. Boil for 8 - 10 minutes until tender, stirring occasionally. Pour into a strainer, rinse with cold water and leave to drain. Add the butter and keep warm.

2. To make the mussel sauce: Prepare and finely chop the onion. Heat the oil and gently fry the onion for about 5 minutes, then add the garlic. Add the white wine and bay leaf. Season.

3. Add the fresh mussels to the sauce. Simmer for about 5 minutes, stirring constantly until the shells open. Discard any unopened ones.

4. Drain the potted mussels. Add the shrimps, tomatoes, mussels

and capers to the sauce. Stir in carefully, bring to the boil and simmer for about 2 minutes.

5. Add the pasta and parsley, mix carefully and serve at once.

Grills in lemon sauce
(6 portions)

Ingredients

500g/1lb/1lb grills

For the sauce:
2 lemons
500ml/18fl oz/2 ¼ cups cream
3x5ml/3tsps/3tsps aquavit
salt and pepper
50g/2oz/4tbs Parmesan cheese, grated

Method

1. Put the pasta into 4 litres/7pts/16 cups of boiling, salted water. Boil for 8 - 10 minutes until tender, stirring occasionally. Pour into strainer, rinse with cold water and leave to drain.

2. To make the sauce: Grate one lemon and reserve grated peel. Remove the white pith from the lemon segments and cut into small pieces. Stir the lemon pieces, and aquavit (if used) through the cream. Bring to the boil and boil for about 5 minutes.

3. Add the juice of the second lemon, return to the boil and boil for another 5 minutes. Season.

4. Mix the pasta with the sauce and stir in the Parmesan cheese. Serve in a flat dish and garnish with the grated lemon peel. Serve with fried breast of chicken or escalopes and green salad.

Macaroni omelette with ham

Ingredients

225g/8oz/¹/₂lb long macaroni
225g/8oz/¹/₂lb boiled ham, diced
100g/4oz/¹/₄lb Cheddar or Ches-
hire cheese, grated
2 eggs
250ml/8fl.oz/1 cup milk
salt and pepper
nutmeg
2x15ml/2tbs/3tbs breadcrumbs

Method

Preheat oven to 190°C/375°F/Gas 5.
1. Break the macaroni in pieces 5 cm (2'') long. Put them into
    1¹/₂litres/2 ¹/₂pts/6 cups boiling, salted water and cook for
    about 15 minutes until tender, stirring occasionally. Pour into
    strainer, rinse with cold water and leave to drain well.

2. Place alternate layers of macaroni, cheese and ham in a greased
    oven-proof dish. The top layer must be macaroni.

3. Beat together the eggs, milk, salt and pepper, nutmeg and pour
    over the macaroni. Sprinkle breadcrumbs over the top.
    Dot with butter and cook in preheated oven for approximately
    40 minutes.
    Serve with fresh lettuce.

Roman macaroni salad

(4 - 6 portions)

Ingredients

175g/6oz/6oz long macaroni
½ a roast chicken
225g/8oz/½lb celery, washed
175g/6oz/6oz gherkins (Dill flavoured)

For the sauce:
175ml/6fl oz/¾ cup sour cream
2x15ml/2tbs/3tbs plain yoghurt
2x15ml/2tbs/3tbs wine vinegar
2x15ml/2tbs/3tbs gherkin liquid
1x15ml/1tbs/2tbs cognac
salt and pepper, and sugar
3x15ml/3tbs/4tbs parsley, chopped

Method

1. Break the macaroni into pieces of 2 cm (1"), put into boiling, salted water. Return to the boil and cook for about 12 minutes until tender, stirring occasionally. Pour into a strainer, rinse with cold water and leave to drain.

2. Remove skin and bones from the chicken and cut into pieces. Drain the gherkins and retain the liquid. Cut the gherkins in half if desired. Cut both celery and gherkins into thin slices.

3. To make the sauce: Mix the sour cream with the yoghurt, vinegar and gherkin liquid. Mix in the cognac and season with salt, pepper and sugar to taste.

4. Stir the sauce through the salad ingredients, allow to be thoroughly absorbed and if necessary season with additional salt, pepper and sugar. Finally stir in the parsley.

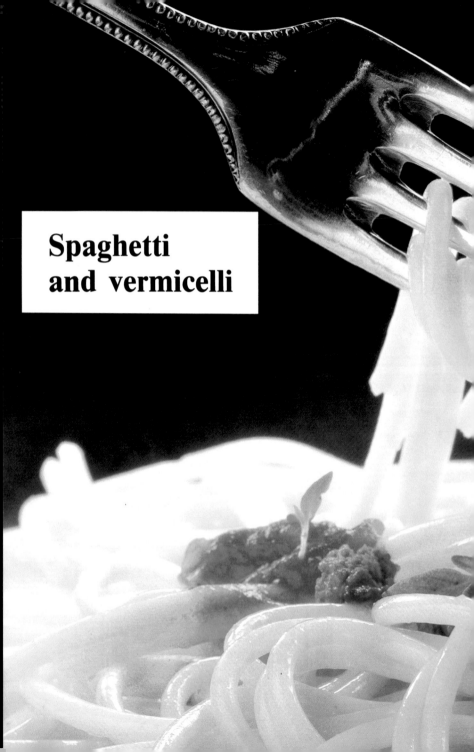

Spaghetti
and vermicelli

Spaghetti bolognese

Ingredients

225g/8oz/½lb spaghetti
1x15ml/1tbs/2tbs salad oil

For the sauce:
2 onions, peeled, chopped
2 cloves garlic, peeled, crushed
2x15ml/2tbs/3tbs olive oil
225g/8oz/½lb minced pork and beef
salt and pepper, and paprika
500g/1lb/1lb tinned tomatoes
75g/3oz/6tbs tomato puree
120ml/4fl oz/½ cup red wine or water
1x5ml/1tsp/1tsp thyme, chopped
1x5ml/1tsp/1tsp basil, chopped
Parmesan cheese, grated

Method

1. Put the spaghetti into 2 litres/3 ½pts/9 cups of boiling, salted water. Add salad oil, bring to the boil and cook for about 10 minutes until tender. Pour into a strainer, rinse with cold water, allow to drain and keep warm.
2. Heat the olive oil and gently fry the onions and garlic. Add the minced meat and cook for about 5 minutes stirring occasionally. Season with salt, pepper and paprika.
3. Add the tinned tomatoes with the juice and lightly mash the tomatoes with a spoon. Add the tomato puree and the red wine or water, stir well, bring to the boil and allow the sauce to simmer for about 15 minutes. Stir in the thyme and basil.
4. Pour the sauce over the spaghetti and sprinkle with Parmesan cheese.

Spaghetti salad torcello

Ingredients

225g/8oz/¹/₂lb spaghetti
175g/6oz/6oz tinned tuna
175g/6oz/5oz sliced ox tongue
2x15ml/2tbs/3tbs capers
lemon slices
lettuce

For the mayonnaise:
1 egg yolk
1x5ml/1tsp/1tsp mustard
1x5ml/1tsp/1tsp anchovy paste
1x15ml/1tbs/2tbs parsley, chopped
1x5ml/1tsp/1tsp sugar
120ml/4fl oz/¹/₂ cup salad oil
salt and pepper
3x5ml/3tsp/3tsp lemon juice

Method

1. Break the spaghetti into small pieces and put into 2 litres/ 3¹/₂pts/9 cups of boiling, salted water. Return to the boil and cook for about 10 - 12 minutes, stirring occasionally. Pour into a strainer, rinse with cold water and leave to drain well.
2. Drain the tinned tuna and break into pieces. Cut the tongue into strips and add with the capers to the tuna and spaghetti.
3. To make the mayonnaise: Beat the egg yolk with the mustard, anchovy paste, lemon juice, salt, pepper and sugar until it is a thick paste. Stir in the salad oil a little at a time.
   Stir in the parsley and pour the mayonnaise over the salad.
4. Mix and leave until it is well absorbed. Season the salad with salt, pepper and sugar to taste.

If desired, wash, drain and dry some lettuce leaves and lay them in a serving dish. Arrange the spaghetti salad on top and garnish with parsley and lemon slices.

Spaghetti with mussels

Ingredients

1kg/2 ¼lbs/2 ¼lbs fresh mussels
120ml/4fl oz/½ cup olive oil
3 cloves garlic, peeled, crushed
1 kg/2¼lbs/2¼lbs tomatoes, blanched, skinned, diced
salt and pepper
2x15ml/2tbs/3tbs parsley, chopped
500g/1lb/1lb spaghetti

Method

1. Wash the mussels several times, brush them thorougly and keep rinsing until the water stays clear. (Mussels that open during washing are not edible.) Heat 3x15ml/3tbs/4tbs of the oil in a pan.

2. Put in the mussels, put a lid on the pan and continue to heat until the mussels open up. Remove from shells and retain the liquid.

3. Heat the remaining oil in a pan and add the garlic, mussels and mussel liquid. Bring to the boil and allow the liquid to reduce.

4. Stir tomatoes into the mussel mixture. Season and allow to boil for about 5 minutes. Stir in the parsley.

5. Put the spaghetti into 3 litres/5½pts/12 cups of boiling, salted water. Return to the boil and cook for about 12 minutes until tender. Pour through a strainer, rinse with cold water and leave to drain.

6. Stir half the sauce through the spaghetti, heat gently and serve the other half separately.

Spaghetti carbonara

(2 persons)

Ingredients

175g/6oz/6oz spaghetti
1x15ml/1tbs/2tbs salad oil
100g/4oz/¾lb streaky bacon, derinded, diced
1x15ml/1tbs/2tbs butter
150ml/4fl oz/¼pt sour cream
salt and pepper
nutmeg, grated
1x5ml/1tsp/1tsp parsley or basil, chopped
Parmesan cheese, grated

Method

1. Put spaghetti into 1 ½ litres/2 ½pts/6 cups of boiling, salted water. Return to the boil and cook for about 8 minutes so that it is not quite cooked. Pour into a strainer, rinse with cold water and leave to drain.
2. Heat the butter and fry the bacon. Stir in the sour cream and bring to the boil briefly. Season with salt, pepper and nutmeg.
3. Add the spaghetti and heat whilst stirring. Stir in the parsley or basil and sprinkle with Parmesan cheese.

Spaghetti salad

(6 - 8 persons)

Ingredients

225g/8oz/½lb spaghetti
350g/12oz/¾lb Italian salami
500g/1lb/1lb tinned peas and carrots

For the sauce:
120ml/4fl oz/½ cup vegetable liquid

(from the tinned peas and carrots)
3x15ml/3tbs/4tbs salad oil
5x15ml/5tbs/6tbs wine vinegar
1x5ml/1tsp/1tsp paprika
1x2.5ml/¹⁄₂tsp/¹⁄₂tsp mustard
salt and pepper
pinch of ground thyme

Spaghetti salad

Method

1. To make the salad: Break the spaghetti into finger-length pieces and put into 1 ½ litres/2 ½ pts/6 cups of boiling, salted water. Return to the boil and cook for about 12 minutes until tender, stirring occasionally. Pour into a strainer, rinse with cold water and leave to drain.

2. Remove the skin from the salami and cut into pieces. Drain the tinned carrots and peas, retaining the liquid. Cut the carrots into pieces.

3. To make the sauce: Mix vegetable liquid with the salad oil, vinegar, paprika and mustard. Season and stir in a little thyme.

4. Pour the sauce over the salad, mix and leave for 10 minutes. If required, add additional salt, pepper and paprika to taste.

Sharkfin soup taifun

Ingredients

1 tin of sharkfin soup
3x15ml/3tbs/4tbs pumpkin (from
a jar or tin)
2x15ml/2tbs/3tbs plain yoghurt
ground ginger
cayenne pepper

Method

1. Prepare the soup according to the instructions on the tin.
2. Cut the pumpkin into small pieces. Mix with yoghurt and season with ginger and cayenne to taste.
3. Pour the soup into preheated cups or bowls. Pieces of the remaining pumpkin may be added to each portion.

Florentine spaghetti

Ingredients

500g/1lb/1lb frozen spinach in white sauce
1x15ml/1tbs/2tbs butter

Sharkfin soup taifun

2 onions, peeled
225g/8oz/½lb spaghetti
salad oil
75g/3oz/6tbs streaky bacon, derinded, diced
350g/12oz/¾lb mild flavoured Continental sausage
Parmesan cheese, grated

Method

1. Thaw the spinach at room temperature. Melt the butter. Chop 1 onion and fry in the butter until transparent.
   Add the spinach and simmer for 5 minutes.
2. Put the spaghetti into 2 litres/3 ½pts/9 cups of boiling, salted water. Add 1x15ml/1tbs/2tbs of salad oil. Bring to the boil and cook for about 8 minutes so that the spaghetti is not completely cooked, stirring occasionally. Pour into a strainer and rinse with warm water. Leave to drain, then mix with the spinach and keep warm.
3. Heat 1x15ml/1tbs/2tbs salad oil and fry bacon. Slice the remaining onion and add to the bacon. Allow to brown lightly and stir through the spinach and spaghetti mixture.
4. Skin the sausage and cut into thin slices. Heat 2x15ml/2tbs/3tbs of salad oil and fry the sausage slices, then lay them on top of the spinach and spaghetti mixture. Sprinkle with Parmesan cheese.

Colourful Italian spaghetti

Ingredients

225g/8oz/½lb spaghetti
500g/1lb/1lb summer vegetables (frozen)
225g/8oz/½lb tinned sweetcorn
3x15ml /3tbs/4tbs butter
50g/2oz/4tbs streaky bacon, in one slice, derinded, diced
1 clove garlic, peeled, crushed
500g/1lb/1lb breast of chicken
1 large onion, peeled, diced
salt and pepper, ground coriander
2x15ml/2tbs/3tbs parsley, chopped

Method

1. Break the spaghetti into finger-length pieces and put into 1 ½ litres/2 ½pts/6 cups of boiling, salted water. Return to the boil and cook for 8 - 10 minutes until tender, stirring occasionally. Pour into a strainer, rinse with cold water and leave to drain.
2. Thaw the vegetables at room temperature. Drain the sweetcorn.
3. Melt the butter and fry the bacon with the garlic. Wash and dry the breast of chicken and cut into strips. Fry the onion together with the chicken in the bacon fat for about 10 minutes. Remove from the pan and keep warm.
4. Simmer the thawed vegetables in the fat for about 10 minutes. Add the chicken and spaghetti to the vegetables and season with salt, pepper and coriander. Heat for 10 minutes and stir in the parsley.

Colourful Italian spaghetti

Italian spaghetti salad

Ingredients

For the salad:
150g/5oz/5oz spaghetti
2 apples, peeled, cored and quartered
3 gherkins
175g/6oz/6oz cooked pork in thin slices

For the sauce:
150ml/5fl oz/²⁄₃ cup sour cream
1x15ml/1tbs/2tbs tomato ketchup (catsup)
1x15ml/1tbs/2tbs milk
2x15ml/2tbs/3tbs gherkin liquid
parsley, chopped
salt

Method

1. To make the salad: Put spaghetti into 1 litre/2pts/5 cups of boiling, salted water. Return to the boil and cook for 10 - 12 minutes until tender, stirring occasionally. Pour into a strainer, rinse with cold water and leave to drain.
2. Slice the apples, gherkins and pork into strips and mix with the spaghetti.
3. To make the sauce: Beat together the sour cream, tomato ketchup, milk and gherkin liquid. Stir in the parsley.
4. Pour the sauce over the salad ingredients and leave for 10 minutes. If necessary, season with salt.

Spaghetti with caper sauce

(6 persons)

Ingredients

100g/4oz/¹⁄₄lb capers
6 anchovy fillets
3 cloves of garlic, peeled, crushed

8x15ml/8tbs/10tbs olive oil
5x15ml/5tbs/6tbs lemon juice
400g/14oz/14oz spaghetti

Method

1. Rinse the capers well and leave to drain. Rinse and dry the anchovy fillets. Mix the capers, anchovies and garlic and mash well.
2. Stir the olive oil into the mixture to make a smooth sauce.

Whilst stirring, gradually add the lemon juice.
3. Put the spaghetti into 3 litres/5½pts/12 cups of boiling,
    salted water. Return to the boil and cook for 10 - 12 minutes
    until tender, stirring occasionally. Pour into a strainer, rinse
    with cold water and leave to drain.
4. Put the spaghetti into a warm serving dish and pour the caper
    sauce on top.

Spaghetti with caper sauce

Spaghetti with walnut butter

Ingredients

275g/10oz/10oz spaghetti
75g/3oz/6tbs butter
75g/3oz/6tbs walnuts, chopped
salt

Method

1. Put the spaghetti into 3 litres/5½pts/12 cups of boiling, salted water. Return to the boil and cook for 10 - 12 minutes until tender, stirring occasionally.
2. Melt the butter and fry the walnuts until light brown. Add the spaghetti, stir well and season with salt.
Spaghetti with walnut butter is delicious served with game specialities, steak or roast beef.

Spaghetti with tomato-mussel sauce
(5 - 6 persons)

Ingredients

400g/14oz/14oz spaghetti

For the sauce:
225g/8oz/½lb tomatoes,
blanched, skinned, diced
350g/12oz/¾lb tuna

225g/8oz/½lb mussels (potted)
4 cloves garlic, peeled, crushed
2x15ml/2tbs/3tbs olive oil
salt and pepper
3x15ml/3tbs/4tbs parsley, chopped

Method

1. To make the sauce: Drain the tuna and break into pieces. Drain the mussels and retain the liquid.
2. Heat the olive oil and fry the garlic gently. Add the tomato pieces and fry together with the garlic for about 5 minutes. Add the mussels and tuna and if required, stir through some of the

mussel liquid. Season and stir in the parsley.

3. Put the spaghetti into 3 litres/5½pts/12 cups of boiling, salted water. Return to the boil and cook for about 10 minutes until tender, stirring occasionally. Pour into a strainer, rinse with cold water and leave to drain well.

4. Put the spaghetti into a hot serving dish and pour the tomato-mussel sauce on top.

Spaghetti with tomato-mussel sauce

Vermicelli salad shanghai

(4 - 6 persons)

Ingredients

100g/4oz/¼lb vermicelli
225g/8oz/½lb lean pork
salt and pepper
curry paste
flour
salad oil
225g/8oz/½lb tinned tangerine
segments
175g/6oz/6oz tinned soya beans
225g/8oz/½lb tinned bamboo
shoots, sliced lengthways
225g/8oz/½lb frozen peas
1x15ml/1tbs/1tbs fresh ginger
root, peeled and finely chopped

For the sauce:
2x15ml/2tbs/3tbs salad oil
2x15ml/2tbs/3tbs vinegar
3x15ml/3tbs/4tbs water
salt
2x15ml/2tbs/3tbs soy sauce
2x5ml/2tsp/2tsp curry paste
sambal oelek (piquant
Indonesian sauce)
sugar

Method

1. To make the salad: Put the vermicelli into a bowl and pour boiling water over it. Leave to stand for 3 - 4 minutes, then put into a strainer and rinse with cold water. Leave to drain well and cut through several times with a knife.

2. Cut the pork into strips. Season with salt, pepper and curry paste and dust with flour.

3. Heat the salad oil and fry the pork until golden. Remove from the fat and allow to cool.

4. Put the tangerines, soya beans, bamboo shoots and peas into a strainer to drain and retain the tangerine juice. Cut the bamboo shoots into strips. Add the ginger and 3x15ml/3tbs/4tbs of tangerine juice to the salad.

5. To make the sauce: Mix the salad oil with the vinegar, water, soy sauce and curry and add a dash of sambal oelek.

6. Pour the sauce over the salad and leave for 10 minutes. If required, add more salt, sugar, curry paste and/or sambal oelek.

Chinese vermicelli dish

Ingredients

*15g/½oz/1tbs dried Chinese
mushrooms
350g/12oz/¾lb pork escalope
salt and pepper
soy sauce
100g/4oz/¼lb vermicelli
500g/1lb/1lb leeks
100g/4oz/¼lb celery
175g/6oz/6oz (tinned) soya beans
150g/5oz/5oz (tinned) bamboo shoots
salad oil
120ml/4fl oz/½ cup stock*

Method

1. Pour boiling water over the mushrooms and leave to soak for
   2 - 3 hours until the mushrooms have increased 4 - 5 times in
   size. Prepare and wash the mushrooms and put into boiling,
   salted water. Return to the boil and simmer for about 1 hour.
   Drain and cut into small pieces.

2. Wash and dry the escalope and cut into thin strips. Divide the
   strips into 2 portions and fry each portion separately in
   3x15ml/3tbs/4tbs of salad oil for about 3 minutes.
   Place the cooked meat in a large pan and season with salt,
   pepper and 4x15ml/4tbs/5tbs of soy sauce.

3. Soak the vermicelli in hand-hot water for 4 - 6 minutes and
   then cut into pieces.

4. Prepare the leeks and cut lengthways. Cut into thin strips, wash and drain. Prepare and wash the celery then cut into strips. Drain the soya beans and the bamboo shoots.

5. Heat 2x15ml/2tbs/3tbs salad oil, add the vegetables and the braise for about 5 minutes. Then add the vegetables and the vermicelli to the meat.
Stir in the stock and 120ml/4fl oz/½ cup soy sauce and heat the mixture well.

Filled pastas

Cannelloni with cheese filling

Ingredients

For the filling:
350g/12oz/¾lb full fat
soft cheese
2 eggs, lightly beaten
50g/2oz/4tbs Parmesan cheese,
grated
2x15ml/2tbs/3tbs parsley,
chopped
ground basil
paprika
175g/6oz/6oz cannelloni

For the sauce:
2 onions, peeled, diced
2 cloves garlic, peeled,
crushed
3x15ml/3tbs/4tbs salad oil
500g/1lb/1lb peeled tomatoes
salt and pepper
sugar
ground oregano
100g/4oz/¾lb Gouda cheese,
grated

Method

Preheat oven to 190°C/375°F/Gas 5.

1. To make the filling: Stir together the soft cheese, eggs,
    Parmesan cheese and parsley. Season with ground basil, salt,
    pepper and paprika.

2. Put this mixture into a piping bag and pipe into the cannelloni.
    Place the cannelloni into a greased oven-proof dish.

3. To make the sauce: Heat the salad oil and fry the onion and
    garlic. Chop the tomatoes finely and add to the mixture. Season
    with salt, pepper, sugar and ground oregano. Cook for about 5
    minutes and spread on top of the cannelloni.
    Sprinkle with Gouda cheese. Cook in preheated oven for 30
    minutes.

4. Serve with a salad of fresh peppers, tomatoes and cucumber.

Stuffed noodles

Ingredients

For the noodle dough:
225g/8oz/½lb plain flour
(all purpose flour)
2 eggs
1x2.5ml/½tsp/½tsp salt
3x15ml/3tbs/4tbs water

Filling 1:
100g/4oz/¼lb ham or pieces of
cooked meat
1 egg yolk
2x15g/2tbs/3tbs Cheddar cheese,
grated
2x15ml/2tbs/3tbs milk

Filling 2:
Spinach, cooked and chopped
mushrooms or tomatoes

Method

1. To make the noodle dough: Pour the flour onto the table or pastry board and make a hollow in the centre. Mix 2 eggs with the salt and water and pour into the hollow in the flour.
2. Using some of the flour knead a thick paste, then work in the rest of the flour and knead into a nice smooth dough. If the dough sticks to the fingers, add some more flour.
3. To make filling 1: Stir the ham or cooked meat into the egg yolk, milk and cheese to make a smooth mixture.
4. To make filling 2: Mix the spinach with mushrooms or tomatoes (finely chopped and lightly fried).
   Roll out the dough in small quantities to a thickness of approximately 5mm (¼"). Cut out squares 7.5 cm (3") and place some of the filling on each square.
6. Lightly beat the white of an egg and use to moisten the edges of the squares. Then fold over the corners to make triangles. Press the edges together firmly.
7. Put the triangles into boiling, salted water and boil for about 20 minutes until cooked.

Macaroni butterflies in midsummer night sauce

(5 - 6 persons)

Ingredients

500g/1lb/1lb macaroni butterflies
1x15ml/1tbs/2tbs salad oil

For the sauce:
1 large onion, peeled,
thinly sliced
225g/8oz/¹⁄₂lb tomatoes,
blanched, skinned, diced
225g/8oz/¹⁄₂lb small courgettes
1x5ml/1tsp/1tsp mint, chopped
1 pepper
175 g/6oz/6oz plums
120ml/4fl oz/¹⁄₂ cup olive oil
salt and pepper
1x5ml/1tsp/1tsp basil, chopped

Method

1. Cut the tips off the courgettes and wash and dry them.
    Cut the pepper through the middle and remove the seeds and
    white pith. Wash and dry the pepper. Cut these 2 ingredients
    into small pieces, add tomatoes and onion.
2. Wash and dry the plums, halve them and remove the stones.
    Add to the vegetables. Pour the olive oil over. Season the
    sauce. Stir in the mint and basil.
3. Put the macaroni butterflies into 4 litres/7pts/16 cups of
    boiling, salted water. Add salad oil and return to the boil.
    Cook for about 8 minutes until tender. Pour into a sieve, rinse
    with cold water and leave to drain.
4. Pour the cold sauce over the macaroni and stir well.
    Serve at once.

Tortiglioni with broccoli

Ingredients

225g/8oz/¹/₂lb tortiglioni
275g/6oz/6oz frozen broccoli
150g/5oz/5oz boiled ham, diced
250ml/8fl oz/1 cup milk
1 egg
1x2.5ml/¹/₂tsp/¹/₂tsp cornflour
(cornstarch)
salt
nutmeg, grated
3x15g/3tbs/4tbs mature Gouda cheese, grated
2x15ml/2tbs/3tbs breadcrumbs

Method

Preheat oven to approximately 190°C/375°F/Gas 5.

1. Put the macaroni into 1 ½ litres/2 ½pts/6 cups of boiling, salted water. Bring to the boil and cook for about 8 minutes until done, stirring occasionally. Pour into a strainer, rinse with cold water and leave to drain.

2. Put the broccoli into boiling, salted water and boil for about 5 minutes. Drain and if required, break into small sprigs.

3. Grease an oven-proof dish and place a layer of macaroni in it. Place the broccoli on top of the macaroni and use the ham for the top layer.

4. Mix the milk, egg and cornflour and season with salt and nutmeg. Pour the mixture into the dish.

5. Mix the Gouda cheese with the breadcrumbs and sprinkle on top of the macaroni mixture. Dot with butter and bake in preheated oven for 45-50 minutes until the crust is brown.

Lasagne al forno

Ingredients

14-16 slices of lasagne
1 clove garlic, peeled
1 large onion, peeled, finely chopped
1x15ml/1tbs/2tbs salad oil
225g/8oz/½lb minced pork and beef
3x15ml/3tbs/4tbs tomato puree
salt and pepper

ground rosemary
ground oregano
ground thyme

For the sauce:
150ml/5fl oz/⅔ cup sour cream
120ml/4fl oz/½ cup milk
40g/1 ½oz/3tbs Parmesan cheese, grated

Method

Preheat oven to 200°C/400°F/Gas 6.
1. Place the slices of lasagne one by one in 1 ½ litres/2 ½pts/ 6 cups of boiling, salted water. Bring to the boil and cook for about 2 minutes. Then put the lasagne into cold water and leave to drain.
2. Rub a pan with garlic. Heat the salad oil and gently fry the onion.
3. Add the meat and fry until golden. Stir in the tomato puree and leave to simmer for a while. Season with salt, pepper, rosemary, oregano and thyme.
4. To make the sauce: Mix the sour cream with milk and Parmesan cheese. Cover the base of a greased oven-proof dish with lasagne and then place alternate layers of meat, sauce and lasagne slices in the dish. Finish with a layer of sauce. Dot with butter and cook in preheated oven for 30 minutes.

Tortellini verde with walnuts (5-6 persons)

Ingredients

175g/6oz/6oz shelled walnuts
2 cloves garlic, peeled, crushed
120ml/4fl oz/½ cup olive oil

120ml/4fl oz/½ cup double cream (heavy cream)
salt

2x15ml/2tbs/3tbs marjoram
leaves, chopped
500g/1lb/1lb tortellini verde

Method

1. Chop about ⅔ of the walnuts into small pieces. Heat the olive oil and sauté the garlic. Add the chopped and whole nuts and heat quickly.
2. Reduce the heat and stir in the cream. Season with salt, and stir in the marjoram.
3. Put the tortellini into 3 litres/5½pts/12 cups of boiling, salted water. Return to the boil and cook for 20-30 minutes until tender. Pour into a strainer, rinse with cold water and leave to drain.
4. Put the tortellini into a serving dish and mix with the sauce. Cover and reheat in a moderate oven for 20 minutes.

Tortellini verde with walnuts

Cannelloni Rosanella

(Cannelloni filled with meat)

Ingredients

For the filling:
1 soft bread roll
225g/8oz/½lb minced pork and beef
salt and pepper
ground oregano
ground thyme
225g/8oz/½lb cannelloni

For the sauce:
150ml/5fl oz/⅔ cup sour cream
6x15ml/6tbs/8tbs milk
salt and pepper
basil, chopped
1x15ml/1tbs/2tbs Parmesan cheese, grated

Method

Preheat oven to 190°C/375°F/Gas 5.
1. To make the filling: Soak the roll in cold water, squeeze out well and mix with the minced meat. Season with salt, pepper, oregano and thyme.
2. Fill the cannelloni with the filling using a small spoon. Lay the cannelloni in a greased, flat, oven-proof dish.
3. To make the sauce: Mix the sour cream with milk. Season to taste with the salt, pepper and basil.
4. Pour the sauce over the cannelloni. They must be entirely covered by the sauce. Sprinkle with Parmesan cheese and dot with butter. Cook in preheated oven for 30 minutes.
   Serve with fresh green salad.

Classic lasagne

Ingredients

500g/1lb/1lb lasagne verde

For the filling:
75g/3oz/6tbs butter
350g/12oz/¾lb minced beef
100g/4oz/¼lb celery, cleaned
120ml/4fl oz/½ cup red wine
100g/4oz/4oz tomato puree
2 carrots, scraped
1 onion, peeled, chopped
5 cloves garlic, peeled,
crushed
salt and pepper

For the sauce:
50g/2oz/4tbs butter
50g/2oz/4tbs flour
250ml/8fl oz/1 cup water
250ml/8fl oz/1 cup cream
Parmesan cheese, grated
nutmeg, grated

Method

Preheat oven to 200°C/400°F/Gas 6.

1. Put the lasagne slices one by one into 2 litres/3 ½pts/9 cups boiling, salted water. Boil for approx 2 minutes.
    Put into cold water and leave.
2. To make the filling: Fry the meat, stirring constantly. Chop the celery and cut the carrots into small dice. Add the garlic with all the vegetables to the meat and sauté gently for 5 minutes. Add the red wine and season. Stir in the tomato puree. Cook for further 5 minutes.

3. To make the sauce: Melt the butter, stir in the flour and cook for 2-3 minutes. Add the water and cream and whisk well together. Bring the sauce to the boil and cook gently for about 10 minutes. Season with Parmesan cheese and nutmeg to taste.
4. Place a thin layer of the filling in a well-greased oven-proof dish, then add alternate layers of sauce, lasagne and filling. Finish with a layer of sauce. Sprinkle with Parmesan cheese and dot with butter. Cook in preheated oven for 30 minutes. Serve with a raw vegetable salad.

Cannelloni on spinach

Ingredients

225/8oz/¹/₂lb cannelloni
50g/2oz/4tbs Emmenthal
cheese, grated
1x15ml/1tbs/2tbs salad oil
1 onion, peeled, chopped
500g/1lb/1lb frozen spinach
salt and pepper
nutmeg, grated

For the sauce:
50g/2oz/4 tbs butter
50g/2oz/4tbs flour
350ml/12fl oz/1 ¹/₂ cups milk
120ml/4fl oz/¹/₂ cup cream
salt and pepper
50g/2oz/4tbs Parmesan cheese,
grated

Method

Preheat oven to 190°C/375°F/Gas 5.
1. Heat the salad oil, add onion, and fry lightly. Add the frozen
   spinach (unthawed) and simmer for about 15 minutes. Season
   with salt, pepper and nutmeg. Drain the spinach and put into
   greased oven-proof dish.
2. To make the sauce: Melt the butter and stir in the flour. Cook
   2-3 minutes. Pour in the milk and cream and whisk until
   smooth. Bring the sauce to the boil and cook gently for about
   2 minutes. Season and pour ¹/₃ of the sauce into a jug.
3. Stir in the Emmenthal cheese and pour half of the sauce over
   the spinach.
4. Pipe the other half of the sauce (using an icing bag and nozzle)
   into the cannelloni.
5. Put the filled cannelloni on the spinach. Pour over the rest of
   the sauce. Sprinkle with Parmesan cheese and dot with butter.
   Cook in preheated oven for 30 minutes.
   The cannelloni can be given a golden crust under the grill, to
   save using the oven.

Tortellini cinderella

(for 2 persons)

Ingredients

1 litre/1 ¾ pts/4 ½ cups
beef stock
100g/4oz/¼lb tortellini
1 clove garlic, peeled
150ml/5fl oz/⅔ cup sour cream

2x15ml/2tbs/3tbs milk
salt and pepper
100g/4oz/¼lb boiled ham
1 bunch chives
nutmeg, grated

Method

1. Put the tortellini into the stock and bring to the boil.
    Cook for about 15 minutes, pour through a strainer, rinse with
    cold water and leave to drain.
2. Rub a pan with the garlic. Put the sour cream and milk into
    the pan. Bring to the boil and add the tortellini. Season with
    salt, pepper and nutmeg, and simmer for several minutes.
3. Cut the ham into strips. Wash the chives and chop finely. Add
    with the ham to the tortellini just before serving, and stir in
    carefully.
    Serve with French bread and salad.

Macaroni butterflies with broccoli

Ingredients

225g/8oz/½lb macaroni butterflies
1x15ml/1tbs/2tbs butter
sugar
350g/12oz/¾ lb frozen broccoli
175ml/6fl oz/¾cup sour cream
1 egg yolk
ground pepper
nutmeg, grated

Method

1. Put the macaroni butterflies into 3 litres/5½pts/12 cups boiling, salted water. Boil for about 10 minutes until tender, stirring occasionally. Pour into a strainer, rinse with cold water, drain and keep warm.
2. Bring 500ml/18fl oz/2 ¼ cups water to the boil with the butter and frozen broccoli. Boil for 5-7 minutes until done, drain and retain the vegetable liquid.
3. Cut the broccoli into pieces. Stir carefully through the macaroni and keep warm.
4. Mix the vegetable liquid and the sour cream together. Bring to the boil and allow to reduce a little. Beat the egg yolk into a little of the sauce and stir into the pan. Cook gently until sauce thickens - do not boil. Season with ground pepper and nutmeg.
5. Pour over the broccoli and macaroni and serve at once.
   Serve with boiled ham.

Tortellini cinderella

Cannelloni au gratin

Ingredients

225g/8oz/½lb cannelloni

For the filling:
175g/6oz/6oz frozen spinach
1 small onion, peeled, chopped
1 clove garlic, peeled, crushed
1x15ml/1tbs/2tbs salad oil
1x15ml/1tbs/2tbs butter
225g/8oz/½lb minced beef
2x15kg/2tbs/3tbs Parmesan
cheese, grated
1x15ml/1tbs/2tbs cream
1 egg

For the sauce:
1 onion, peeled
1 clove garlic, peeled, crushed
50g/2oz/4tbs streaky bacon,
de-rinded, diced
1x15ml/1tbs/2tbs salad oil
350ml/12fl oz/1 ½ cups stock
1x15ml/1tbs/2tbs flour
50g/2oz/4tbs tomato puree
ground basil
ground oregano
Cheddar cheese, grated

Method

Preheat oven to 180°C/350°F/Gas 4.

1. To make the filling: Thaw the spinach and drain. Heat the oil and lightly fry the onion and garlic until transparent. Add the spinach and allow it to boil. Put the vegetables into a bowl.

2. Melt the butter and cook the meat, then add it to the spinach. Stir in the Parmesan cheese, the cream and the egg. Season with oregano, salt and pepper.

3. Fill the cannelloni with the spinach and meat mixture.

4. To make the sauce: Heat the salad oil and fry the bacon. Add the onion and garlic and fry gently until transparent. Sprinkle the flour over and fry gently. Stir in the tomato puree and season. Add basil and oregano. Pour in the stock and stir all ingredients well. Bring to the boil and cook for about 10 minutes. Pour a little sauce into a greased, oven-proof dish.

5. Lay the cannelloni in rows and pour the rest of the sauce over the top. Sprinkle with cheese and dot with butter. Put in preheated oven for approx 15 minutes.

Fiesole salad

Ingredients

For the salad:
225g/8 oz/⅟₂lb shell macaroni
2x15ml/2tbs/3tbs salad oil
4 slices cooked pork
salt and pepper
ground sage
40g/1 ½ oz/3tbs capers

For the mayonnaise:
1 egg yolk
1x5ml/1tsp/1tsp mustard
1x15ml/1tbs/2tbs vinegar
salt
1x5ml/1tsp/1tsp sugar
120ml/4fl oz/ ½ cup salad oil
3x15ml/3tbs/4tbs capers liquid
sage

Method

1. To make the salad: Put the macaroni into 2 litres/3 ½ pts/9 cups of boiling, salted water. Boil for about 15 minutes, stirring occasionally. Pour into a strainer, rinse with cold water and leave to drain.
2. Heat the oil. Fry the pork for 5 minutes each side. Season with salt, pepper and sage. Remove from pan, leave to cool and cut into strips. Retaining the liquid, drain the capers.
3. To make the mayonnaise: Mix the egg yolk, mustard, vinegar, salt and sugar to a thick paste. Beat in the salad oil a little at a time. Stir in the caper liquid.
4. Pour the mayonnaise over the salad. Leave for 10 minutes and season.

Cannelloni with broccoli

Ingredients

750g/1 ½lb/1 ½lb frozen can-
nelloni
75g/6oz/6oz salami
150g/5oz/5oz cheese

200ml/⅓pt/⅞cup double cream
nutmeg, grated
500g/1lb/1lb frozen broccoli
melted butter

Method

Preheat oven to 190°C/375°F/Gas 5.
1. Thaw the cannelloni and lay it on a greased, oven-proof dish.
2. Slice the salami. Grate the cheese coarsely. Lay the salami and cheese on the cannelloni and pour the cream over the top.
3. Cook in preheated oven for approx 40 minutes.
4. Bring 1 litre/1 ¾pts/4 ½ cups of water with salt and a little nutmeg to the boil. Put in the broccoli and boil for about 8 minutes. Remove the broccoli from the pan with a skimmer and place on a heated serving dish.
5. Pour melted butter over the broccoli and serve with the cannelloni.

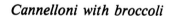

Cannelloni with broccoli

Ravioli

Ingredients

For the dough:
275g/10oz/2 ¼ cups flour
2 eggs, 2 egg whites
2x15ml/2tbs/3tbs salad oil

For the completed ravioli:
50g/2oz/4tbs butter
100g/4oz/ ¼lb Parmesan
cheese, grated
parsley, chopped

For the filling:
salad oil
225g/8oz/ ½lb minced pork and
beef
1 small onion, peeled, diced
1 clove garlic, peeled, crushed
1 medium carrot
2 egg yolks
1x15ml/1tbs/2tbs tomato puree
pinch of ground thyme
salt and pepper

Method

1. To make the dough: Pour flour onto the table or pastry board, and make a hollow in the centre. Beat the eggs with egg whites, ½ of the salad oil and a little salt. Pour into the hollow in the flour and using some of the flour, mix to a thick paste. Working from the centre, knead all the ingredients into a smooth dough. If the dough is sticky, add more flour. Cover the dough with a damp cloth and leave for about 10 minutes.

2. To make filling: Heat remaining salad oil and cook the meat, breaking up any lumps.

3. Grate carrot and add vegetables to minced meat. Fry for about 5 minutes. Stir in egg yolks, puree and thyme. Season.

4. To make the ravioli: Sprinkle ½ of dough with flour, roll out thinly and divide into two. Cover one layer with a damp cloth.

5. Put walnut-sized portions of filling in straight rows on the other layer. Leave a space of about 5 cm (2'') between the portions. With a wet pastry brush paint lines from left to right and from top to bottom between the portions to form little squares.

6. Place the other layer of dough on top and press down firmly

along the wet lines. Cut out the squares with a pastry cutting wheel (see photograph). Lay the ravioli on a sheet of greaseproof paper. Use the remaining dough and filling to make more ravioli.

7. Bring 5 litres/8 ¾pts/1 gal of salted water and 1x15ml/1tbs/2tbs of oil to the boil and boil the ravioli for 8-10 minutes until tender, stirring carefully. Pour into a strainer, leave to drain and put in a preheated dish. Melt butter and pour over the ravioli.

Danish salad

(4-6 persons)

Ingredients

For the salad:
100g/4oz/ ¼lb shell macaroni
2 hardboiled eggs
100g/4oz/ ¼lb boiled ham
275g/10oz/10oz petit pois peas
175g/6oz/6oz tinned asparagus

For the dressing:
3x15ml/3tbs/4tbs salad cream
2x15ml/2tbs/3tbs double cream
4x15ml/4tbs/5tbs vegetable liquid
2x15ml/2tbs/3tbs vinegar
salt and pepper, and sugar

Method

1. To make the salad: Put the macaroni into 1litre/1 ¾pts/4½ cups of boiling, salted water. Boil for about 15 minutes until tender, stirring occasionally. Pour into a strainer, rinse with cold water and leave to drain.

2. Dice the eggs and ham. Cook the peas and asparagus and drain, retaining the vegetable liquid.

3. To make the dressing: Mix the salad cream, cream, vegetable liquid and vinegar together thoroughly. Season with salt, pepper and sugar. Pour over the salad.
Leave for 10 minutes and season if required.

4. To make a more substantial salad, add tinned tuna fish and anchovies, and serve with a crisp green salad.

Spätzle

Spätzle

Ingredients

350g/12oz/ ¾lb flour
4 eggs
1x5ml/1tsp/1tsp salt
12x15ml/12tbs/15tbs water
50g/2oz/4tbs butter

Method

1. Sieve the flour into a bowl. Make a hollow in the middle. Beat the eggs lightly with the salt and water. Pour a little of the mixture into the hollow. Mix with the flour, working from the centre outwards.
2. Gradually add the rest of the mixture. Take care that the dough is not lumpy. Beat the dough until air bubbles appear.
3. Press dough through a special spätzle sieve or a coarse sieve.
4. Put a little at a time into boiling, salted water. Boil until tender. (The spätzle are ready when they rise to the surface.) Bring to the boil again. Pour into a strainer, rinse with cold water and leave to drain. Melt the butter and mix through the spätzle. Serve hot.

Spätzle with cheese and herbs

Ingredients

350g/12oz/ ¾lb flour
4 eggs
1x5ml/1tsp/1tsp salt
12x15ml/12tbs/15tbs water
150g/5oz/5oz Emmenthal cheese,
grated
3x15ml/3tbs/4tbs mixed herbs,
chopped
50g/2oz/4tbs butter

Method

1. Sieve the flour into a bowl. Make a hollow in the middle. Lightly beat the eggs with salt and water. Pour some of this mixture into the hollow in the flour. Mix with the flour working from the centre outwards.
2. Gradually add the rest of the mixture. Take care that the dough is not lumpy. Mix in the cheese and herbs.
3. Press the dough through a special spätzle sieve or a coarse sieve.
4. Put a little at a time into boiling, salted water. Boil until tender (the spätzle are done when they float to the surface). Bring to the boil again, then pour the spätzle into a strainer, rinse with cold water and leave to drain. Melt the butter and mix into the spätzle.

Rye Spätzle

Ingredients

500g/1lb/1lb rye flour
4 eggs
1x5ml/1tsp/1tsp salt

250ml/5fl oz/1 cup water
1x15ml/1tbs/2tbs salad oil
50g/2oz/4tbs butter

Method

1. Sieve the flour into a bowl. Make a hollow in the middle. Beat the eggs with the salt, water and oil. Pour the mixture into the hollow in the flour.
2. Working from the centre mix with the flour, then gradually add the rest of the mixture. Take care that the dough is not lumpy. Beat the dough until air bubbles appear.
3. Press the dough through a special spätzle sieve or a coarse sieve.
4. Put a little at a time into boiling, salted water. Boil until tender (the spätzle are ready when they float to the surface). Bring to the boil again, then pour into a strainer and rinse with cold water. Melt the butter and mix into the spätzle. Serve Rye Spätzle with pork steaks and fresh summer vegetables.

Veal rolls with sour sauce

Ingredients

4 thin veal escalopes
(approx 100g/4oz/ ¼lb each)
salt and pepper
4 slices of ham
(approx 50g/2oz/2oz each)
2x15ml/2tbs/3tbs flour
4 hardboiled eggs
40g/1 ½oz/3tbs butter
1 onion peeled, chopped
250ml/8fl oz/1 cup stock
450ml/ ¾pt/2 cups sour cream

Method

1. Rinse and dry the escalopes and if necessary flatten them. Season with salt and pepper.

2. Lay a slice of ham and a hardboiled egg on each escalope. Roll up the meat from the short end and fasten the rolls with cocktail sticks or tie them with kitchen string.

3. Heat butter and fry the rolls until golden brown on all sides. Add onion and fry with the meat.

4. Gradually add half the warm stock. Turn the rolls occasionally and simmer for about 20 minutes until cooked. Remove the cocktail sticks or kitchen string and keep the rolls hot.

5. Pour the gravy through a sieve, add remaining stock and bring to the boil. Mix in sour cream and flour. Thicken the sauce with this mixture and season.
Heat the rolls for 5 more minutes in the sauce. Serve hot with spätzle.

Gypsy Spätzle

Ingredients

350g/12oz/ ¾lb flour
3 eggs
75g/3oz/6tbs paprika powder

15x15ml/15tbs/18tbs water
50g/2oz/4tbs butter

Method

1. Sieve the flour into a bowl. Make a hollow in the middle. Beat the eggs lightly with the paprika powder and water. Pour some of the mixture in the hollow and working from the centre, mix with the flour.
2. Gradually add the rest of the mixture. Take care that the dough is not lumpy. Beat the dough until air bubbles appear.
3. Press the dough through a special spätzle sieve or coarse sieve.
4. Put a little at a time into boiling, salted water. Boil until tender (the spätzle are cooked when they rise to the surface). Bring to the boil again, pour into a strainer and rinse with cold water. Melt the butter and mix through the spätzle. Serve Gypsy Spätzle with veal and fresh lettuce.

Tomato Spätzle

Ingredients

350g/12oz/ ¾lb flour
4 eggs
1x5ml/1tsp/1tsp salt

4x15ml/4tbs/5tbs tomato puree
10x15ml/10tbs/12tbs water
50g/2oz/4tbs butter

Method

1. Sieve the flour into a bowl and make a hollow in the middle. Beat the eggs lightly with the salt, tomato puree and water. Pour some of the mixture in the hollow in the flour.
2. Working from the centre, mix with the flour, then gradually add the rest of the mixture. Take care that the dough is not lumpy. Beat the dough until air bubbles appear.

3. Press the dough through a special spätzle sieve or a coarse sieve.
4. Put a little at a time into boiling, salted water. Boil until tender (the spätzle are ready when they float to the surface). Bring to the boil again, pour into a strainer, rinse with cold water and leave to drain. Melt the butter and mix through the spätzle. Serve Tomato Spätzle with veal ragoût.

Tomato Spätzle

Green Spätzle

Ingredients

175g/6oz/6oz frozen spinach, chopped
350g/12oz/ ¾lb flour
4 eggs

1x5ml/1tsp/1tsp salt
12x15ml/12tbs/15tbs water
50g/2oz/4tbs butter

Method

1. Thaw the spinach and drain. Sieve the flour into a bowl. Make a hollow in the middle. Beat the eggs lightly with the salt and water. Pour some of the mixture in the hollow in the flour.
2. Working from the centre, mix with the flour, then gradually add the rest of the mixture. Take care that the dough is not lumpy. Beat the dough until air bubbles appear, then stir the spinach through the dough.
3. Press the dough through a special spätzle sieve or a coarse sieve.
4. Put a little at a time into boiling, salted water. Boil until tender (the spätzle are done when they float to the surface). Boil again, then pour into a strainer, rinse with cold water and leave to drain. Melt the butter and mix through the spätzle.

Parsley Spätzle

Ingredients

50g/2oz/6tbs parsley
3 eggs
350g/12oz/ ¾lb flour
1x5ml/1tsp/1tsp salt

pepper
120ml/4fl oz/ ½ cup water
50g/2oz/4tbs butter

Method

1. Wash, drain and chop the parsley. Beat the eggs and add the parsley. Add flour, salt, pepper and water.
2. Mix all ingredients well, taking care that there are no lumps.

Beat the dough until air bubbles appear. Press the dough through a special spätzle sieve or a coarse sieve.

3. Put a little at a time into boiling, salted water. Cook until tender (the spätzle are done when they rise to the surface). Boil again and then pour into a strainer. Rinse with cold water and leave to drain. Melt the butter and mix through the spätzle. Serve Parsley Spätzle with goulash.

Parsley Spätzle

Cheese Spätzle

Ingredients

350g/12oz/ ¾lb flour
4 eggs
1x5ml/1tsp/1tsp salt
12x15ml/12tbs/15tbs water
150g/5oz/5oz Emmenthal cheese,
grated
4 onions, peeled
50g/2oz/4tbs lard

Method

1. Sieve the flour into a bowl and make a hollow in the middle.

2. Working from the centre, stir the egg mixture into the flour. Gradually add the rest of the mixture, taking care that the dough does not become lumpy. Beat the dough until air bubble appear. Press the dough through a special spätzle sieve or a coarse sieve.

3. Put a little at a time into boiling, salted water. Return to the boil, cook until tender (the spätzle are done when they rise to the surface). Boil again, then pour into a strainer, rinse with cold water and leave to drain.

4. Put the spätzle into an oven-proof dish to keep warm. Sprinkle each layer of spätzle with some of the Emmenthal cheese. The top layer should consist of cheese.

5. If required 4 onions can be cut into rings. Melt the lard, fry th onion rings until golden and arrange them over the cheese spätzle before serving.
   Serve with mixed green salad.

Contents

Index

Broccoli
  tortiglioni, 58
  macaroni butterflies, 68
  cannelloni, 72

Cannelloni
  with cheese filling, 54
  Rosanella, 62
  on spinach, 66
  au gratin, 70
  with broccoli, 72

Cheese
  macaroni, 16
  cannelloni, 54
  spätzle and herbs, 80
  spätzle, 88

Fettucine
  with smoked salmon salad, 12
  au gratin, 24

Lasagne
  al forno, 60
  classic, 64

Macaroni
  salad, 10
  with garlic and olive oil, 14
  with piquant cheese, 16
  with paprika-fig sauce, 18
  buttered, 20
  vegetable soup, 22
  omelette with ham, 30
  Roman salad, 31
  butterflies in midsummer
    night sauce, 56
  butterflies with broccoli, 68

Noodles
  Tyrolienne, 14
  home made, 24
  stuffed, 55

Salads
  Italian, 11
  Venetian, 20
  Fiesole, 72
  Danish, 76

Spaghetti
  bolognese, 34
  salad torcello, 35
  with mussels, 36
  salad, 38
  Florentine, 40
  carbonara, 42
  colourful Italian, 42
  Italian salad, 44
  with caper sauce, 44
  with walnut butter, 46
  with tomato-mussel sauce, 46

Spätzle
  spätzle, 80
  with cheese and herbs, 80
  rye, 81
  Gypsy, 84
  tomato, 84
  green, 86
  parsley, 86
  cheese, 88

Tagliatelle
  and chervil sauce, 6
  with mussels, 7
  with seafood, 26

© MCMLXXXIV by Ceres-Verlag Rudolf August Oetker
KG, Bielefeld
All rights reserved.
English language edition
© MCMLXXXV Invader Ltd.,
10 Eastgate Square, Chichester, England.
All rights reserved. No part of this publication may be re-
produced, stored in a retrieval system or transmitted, in any
form or by any means, electronic, mechanical, photocopy-
ing, recording or otherwise, without the prior permission of
the copyright owner.
ISBN 1-85129-031-1
Printed in Belgium.